Wholesaling Lease Options

Discover the Fastest & Easiest Way to Make Money in Real Estate Today

Joe McCall

Copyright 2018 Joe McCall

ALL RIGHTS RESERVED. This book contains material protected under International and Federal Copyright Laws and Treaties. Any unauthorized reprint or use of this material is prohibited. No part of this book may be reproduced or transmitted in any form or by any means, electronic or mechanical, including photocopying, recording, or by any information storage and retrieval system, without express written permission from the author/publisher.

ISBN: 978-1-64184-023-1

CONTENTS

Introduction 1

Chapter 1: Finding The Seller 13

Chapter 2: Making The Offer 29

Chapter 3: Finding The Tenant-Buyer 55

Chapter 4: Putting It All Together
(How To Make A Full-Time Income
Wholesaling Lease Options) 67

Chapter 5: Work Smarter Not Harder -
Partner With Me 81

About The Author 89

INTRODUCTION

"What do Wholesaling Lease Options make possible for me?"

That's the question I want to encourage you to ask yourself day after day, week after week, and month after month as we start down this journey of Wholesaling Lease Options together.

What does more money make possible? What does more flexibility in your day-to-day schedule make possible? What does having control over the quality of your own life make possible?

There's a reason you picked this book in the first place. Maybe it's one or even all of those things listed above. Maybe it's something else. Maybe it's your entrepreneurial spirit wanting to try something new.

Whether you want to build a comfy side hustle or grow a lucrative business in Wholesaling Lease Options, I want you to know that it is possible to make more money in just a few sales doing Wholesaling Lease Options than you make in a month (or in some cases, a year) at your current vocation.

WHAT HAS WHOLESALING LEASE OPTIONS MADE POSSIBLE FOR ME?

I'm the poster child for what Wholesaling Lease Options can make possible. I'm just a regular guy. In fact, given my name Joe McCall, you might even think of me as an "average Joe". In my case, that means being an avid family guy spending quality time with my wife and kids — at the zoo, on the golf course, or in the swimming pool. I'm a man of faith and constantly amazed by Jesus Christ and how awesome he is. Family and God come first.

Like any husband or father worth his salt, I devoted myself to win at work so that we could have the life we always dreamed of. World travel was always a high priority for my life, even as far back as college. I graduated from Iowa State University with a degree in Civil Engineering and working for a large engineering company afforded me plenty of travel.

Eventually I met my wife and we settled down in Kansas City. A few years into the job I was transferred to San Francisco for a two-year assignment. Since two years isn't that long of a time to be away, my wife and I decided to rent out the house and hire a property management company to tend to it rather than sell. Huge mistake!

I'm not knocking property managers across the board. It's just that this company in particular was flat out awful. They had so many fees that if you looked up "nickel and diming" in the dictionary you might find their company logo in the definition.

Moreover, my tenant was horrible. He must have been a plant from the property management company because that's the only way I can explain why he kept breaking things and never paid the rent on time. This, of course, allowed the property management company to send me more bills than I knew how to pay for. One time they charged me $65 an hour to fix a leaky faucet — that I could have fixed myself in less than 15 minutes. It was a total nightmare.

Everything changed when my two-year assignment was shortened after just 10 months. I was asked to move back to Kansas City, but unfortunately my nightmare tenant still had two months left on the lease. We endured those final two months and decided to cut ties with the house and sell it — only to realize the property management company had the rights to become the listing agent because of our contract. They managed to cut yet another juicy fee for themselves.

Yours truly, Joe McCall, officially became the world's biggest hater of rental real estate. Fortunately I had a friend who did a lot of rental properties and he recommended I read Robert Kiyosaki's famous book, Rich Dad, Poor Dad. That book showed me what could be possible as a result of real estate. I found myself "devouring" any kind of material I could about real estate and eventually I found another book by Robert Shemin called Secrets of the Millionaire Landlord.

It was this book that opened me up to the concept of "tenant buyers" and Shemin described them in his chapter on lease options. A tenant buyer is someone who rents (like a tenant) but plans to eventually buy the place they are renting. Tenant-buyers can be great because they're more likely to take care of the rental — they won't want to destroy the place they're planning to buy later on. To get tenant-buyers, you have to do a "lease option" which is something I'll explain in detail throughout the rest of this book.

Long story short, in 2005 I started taking real estate investing seriously and joined a coaching program to the tune of $13,000. I had the bright idea of putting it all on my credit card and strangely this didn't bother my wife very much. In fact, she was happy and excited and we both thought the program was going to be incredible.

The program indeed delivered on everything it advertised. It provided great content in the form of books, marketing tools, and coaching calls. There was one problem: I didn't see any results. The reason? I didn't work. I never finished the homework and always found an excuse for not doing it. I'm positive

I would have seen results if I actually put in the work, but looking back this program at least made me aware of the importance of two key components I'm going to share with you in this book: marketing and automation.

A few years later in 2007, I finally took action and started making actual offers on real estate properties — mostly to take over existing mortgages. I built a portfolio of about 6 to 8 homes but it turns out these weren't very good investments. There simply wasn't enough cash flow — each house only netted about $150 each.

Odd as it may sound (call it ignorance) I wasn't very worried. I thought the cash flow would increase dramatically in 15 years after the mortgages were paid off and I would own the homes free-and-clear. All I had to do was hold steady.

I made some foolish assumptions at the time. For example, I assumed that real estate never depreciates. I assumed that tenant-buyers would actually buy their homes. I assumed tenants would actually pay their rent on time. Boy, was I wrong. With each of these bad assumptions, I had left out one very important and unpredictable factor: life.

My investments ballooned to about 14-16 homes and eventually I hit the limit on how many mortgages I could get from banks. Ever the bulldog, I found a way to overcome these limits by getting into lease options and, believe it or not, I felt good about where I was. I really started to believe I could make a go of this whole real estate thing.

In hindsight, this was the calm before the storm because along came the great recession of 2008. The crash completely exposed my lack of preparation in the fundamentals of real estate investing. I found myself scrambling to find the money to pay those 14 to 16 mortgages on time, especially because I didn't want to wreck other people's credit. Each seller was still tied to the house through the deal we set up, so if I dropped the ball on the mortgage payment the seller would suffer — and probably take me to court, too.

If this sounds frightening, it was. A few people threatened to sue me. I was drowning in tons of debt. Somehow I always found a way to pay the mortgages on time. Unfortunately there were many months that I didn't have enough money to pay my own mortgage.

And, believe it or not, I wasn't even a full-time real estate investor yet — I was still working a full-time job 50 to 60 hours a week!

THE STRATEGY THAT CHANGED EVERYTHING: WHOLESALING LEASE OPTIONS

When 2009 came around, I stumbled into a strategy that helped turn my entire life around. No, it wasn't a silver bullet, but it was very powerful strategy. This book, and my entire coaching business, is based on this strategy: Wholesaling Lease Options.

When you do a "lease option" on a house, you have a "lease" with an "option" to buy the house within a certain period of time. Rockefeller once said, "The secret to success is to own nothing, but control everything." Lease options are the ultimate form of control without ownership.

You get all the benefits of controlling an incredibly valuable piece of real estate (cash now, cash flow, cash flow), without actually "owning" it. Since you don't actually "own" the property, and you don't have to use any of your own money or credit to do a lease option, you have very little risk in the deal.

For now, let me give you a broad overview of the strategy on how to make this work. Wholesaling lease options involves three critical components: Marketing, Automation and Delegation

Please understand that you are not really in the real estate business — you are in the marketing business. This is the first and most important concept you must understand.

Once you get clear on marketing, you can move into automation. Automation is just a big word that means having systems in place that run by themselves. When you automate your marketing in the way I'll describe, you won't have to push, strive, or claw to make things happen.

Delegation means you outsource the work to others who support your vision and do the work for you. Let me give you an example of how this all fits together.

I recently flipped six lease option deals in three different markets all while traveling around the country in my RV. By "traveling" I mean I was really traveling — I wasn't sitting in the RV on my laptop working twelve hours a day and then taking a walk outside. I was fully present in the sights and experiences of travel. How?

First, I had a virtual assistant (or "VA" for short) in the Philippines send my emails and take care of my marketing. Second, I had a local wholesaler on the ground in each of those three markets. These guys took leads, talked to sellers, and ultimately sold each house. Finally, I had some realtors helping with the sales and some local assistants managing it all.

The entire system took some time to set up, but once it was the whole thing was like clockwork.

OTHER "AVERAGE JOES" LIKE ME HAVE MADE THIS WORK, TOO.

Ronnie Jones in St. Louis is a student in my apprentice program and made $25,093 on just one deal based on the strategy outlined in this book. Ronnie never visited the property in the deal, nor did he ever speak with the buyers or sellers directly. Instead, he relied on an acquisition manager, a VA, and a few others to do all the "heavy lifting" for him. Ronnie wasn't a one-shot wonder, either. He's still in the game and his success is evident: "small deals" for him are now those where he only makes $5,000 to $10,000.

Is Ronnie just an exception? Maybe, but then how do you explain Murat — another guy who's "on fire" with Wholesaling Lease Options. Murat is in Rochester, NY (near the Great Lakes) and about a thousand miles away from Ronnie. It has nothing to do with geography because these strategies work in any market.

Murat's first Wholesaling Lease Options deal netted him $6,550. The property was in Buffalo, about an hour's drive from Murat — not that he ever drove there. He did the entire deal without ever visiting the house. Murat has continued to use my strategies in places like Alabama and Louisiana with very nice houses, some of which are even in gated communities.

He'll be the first to tell you that there were days he felt like giving up. What I noticed after interviewing him was his hunger to learn. Before we met, he took two other somewhat satisfactory courses on lease options. The breakthrough came on the third try when we worked together in my Wholesaling Lease Options 3.0 course.

Don't worry, this book isn't going to turn into some big commercial for my program because the

X-factor when it comes to thriving in Wholesaling Lease Options is you. It's the action you take. It's the seriousness by which you immerse yourself in the content in order to rewire your mindset to learn new skills so you can create new pathways to wealth. You'll learn important marketing strategies like how to present yourself as a professional and not like a "fly by night" investor, as well as how to "talk the talk" and develop your self-confidence so people line up to work with you. (Remember I said earlier that marketing is the most critical component?)

I hope you're feeling inspired. If you aren't, I hope you'll at least consider the question I asked you at the start of this section just one more time: What do Wholesaling Lease Options make possible for me?

Life has come full circle now. I've been an active investor for years and I'm as passionate about it today as when I first started because of all the things it has made possible for me and my family. While I love flipping deals (I've personally done over 100 of them) I also love teaching and coaching others to flip deals, too. If you add up the total number of deals my students have flipped, the number skyrockets into the thousands. I've lost track of how many times I've received a card in the mail or a testimonial into my inbox telling me about how a student flipped a deal that changed his or her life.

I KNOW WHOLESALING LEASE OPTIONS CAN DO THE SAME FOR YOU.

As you read this book, I encourage you to keep an open mind and be a voracious learner. Immerse yourself in this content. Lean into the testimonials of "average Joe's" that have made $5,000, $10,000, $15,000 or more with just one deal.

If you're more of an auditory learner or have a daily commute, shut off the news or sports talk radio and tune into my Real Estate Investing Mastery podcast. There are over 600 episodes with listeners tuning in from over 170 different countries, and it's absolutely free. Just login to iTunes, type in my name "Joe McCall", find the show, and subscribe.

Finally, if you'd like a deep-dive into the content presented in this book, you can sign up for a full-length masterclass online at www.WLOwebinar.com. I've been told the class alone is worth hundreds of dollars, but you can view it for free. You'll also get information on the aforementioned Wholesaling Lease Options 3.0 program and how you can work with me directly.

I'm going to be honest and realistic with you because you deserve the truth. There will be tough days. There will be moments when you feel like giving up. You will really wonder if this will all be worth it. When you experience those times I want you to remember the simple question I asked you at the start of this section: "What do Wholesaling Lease Options make possible for me?".

If you're ready to start learning, fasten your proverbial seatbelt as we head into our first Chapter Finding the Seller.

1
FINDING THE SELLER

"Success is sequential, not simultaneous."

— Gary Keller

There is one single unchanging concept that you must lay hold of in order to experience the benefits, freedom, and wealth that Wholesaling Lease Options can give you: success is sequential, not simultaneous.

The number one mistake I see people make when entering this space is thinking that everything will just happen at once, or worse, that they need to do everything at once. Opportunities will never be capitalized upon if you are in a constant state of overwhelm. You must stay cool, calm, and collected. This is something that I will remind you of throughout the course of this book.

WHAT IS A LEASE OPTION?

Before we go any further, we need to define what a Lease Option is. When you do a "Lease Option" on a house, you have a "Lease" with an "Option" to buy the house within a certain period of time. Lease Options are the ultimate form of control without ownership.

In a Lease Option, you get all the benefits of controlling a valuable piece of real estate (cash now, cash flow, cash flow), without actually "owning" it. Since you do not actually "own" the property, and you do not have to use any of your own money or credit to do a lease option, you have very little risk in the deal.

KEEP IT SIMPLE

You have placed a measure of trust in me to guide you into the world of Wholesaling Lease Options, so I am going to show you the exact process that I follow to this day to successfully close deals. This is the 4-step process you will follow. While the details within may change depending on the market, buyer, or seller, this is the proven path to profit:

1. Find The Seller
2. Make An Offer
3. Find A Tenant-Buyer
4. Close the Deal

In this chapter, we will cover the four steps you need to take in order to find a seller. In the sales world, we call this prospecting. All of prospecting boils down to this simple premise: find the person with the problem. The key word here is "find" — you are going to have to do a bit of legwork. Do not be discouraged. After you do it once, you will find it much easier to do the next time around, and with each subsequent endeavor your skills will improve.

To do this, you need to take four steps:

1. Market Research
2. Pinpoint Key Zip Codes
3. Marketing - Online
4. Marketing - Offline

1. DO YOUR MARKET RESEARCH

The word research has a funny effect on people. Research papers were not my forte in school so I never liked the word, but now I love it because doing the proper research all but guarantees the best use of my time, energy, and investments.

It is time to do your homework but do not despair — I am not talking about toiling away for countless hours sifting through hundreds of records. The internet makes this very easy.

Your first step is to find out where the nice homes are. Next, you should look up median homes so you can identify the minimum rents you want to work with. Finally, you should look up where in-demand homes are.

The key here is to find a home that is a combination of these things: a nice home that is in-demand. Working with this kind of property makes selling so much faster and easier. You will never sit around nervously biting your nails in anticipation of a sale if you find a home that is nice and in-demand.

A REAL LIFE EXAMPLE OF HOW TO RUN YOUR RESEARCH

The first and most useful tool you will use is Trulia's Heat Maps, which can be found on trulia.com. A heat map is simply a tool that visually displays data on a map. You have likely seen something like this when looking at population statistics, or if you are a sports fan, on broadcasts where they show the places on the court that a basketball team has taken shots from.

It is no different here. Trulia will give you this information for free. In this instance, I decided to look up Shelby County in Tennessee. I go to Google (not Trulia), type in the phrase "Shelby County Tennessee heat map" and look for the result provided by Trulia. Then, sort the findings by "popularity".

This will tell you the most popular ZIP Codes that people search for in that county.

Another thing you need to do is search median home prices. To do this, simply Google "median home price, Shelby County Tennessee." If you do this, the result you want to click on is from the real estate site Zillow (zillow.com).

At the time of this writing, Google states the median home price for Shelby County is about $109,300. This sounds like a low figure compared to the rest of the country, but that does not matter as much as you finding a property that is somewhere near the median home price range. The goal here is to be average. You want to deal with homes that are smack in the middle of the bell curve.

The reason you want to be average is because those are the homes that sell the most. In any market, the hardest homes to sell are the expensive ones (because of price) and the cheapest ones (because the home may be rundown or in a bad neighborhood). These types of homes are on the edges of the bell curve. Mathematicians would describe these homes as "outliers".

I cannot emphasize this point enough. Most people who struggle to flip deals do so because they picked outlier homes. Statistics have shown that 68% of all homes sold in a market are within about 34% of the middle. This should be a guide for you.

Target homes that are no more than 30 - 40% above or below the median value.

What about the average price range for a home? My advice is to avoid anything under $100,000. With our Shelby County example, that means focusing on homes somewhere between $100,000 to $175,000.

2. PINPOINT KEY ZIP CODES

The next step is to go to Trulia's heat map and find the most popular zip codes that contain homes in that price range. In Shelby County, those zip codes would be 38016, 38125, and 38018. Generally speaking, Trulia will give you somewhere between five and ten zip codes. Your goal is to be a big fish in those small ponds.

I know this sounds almost too simple, but that is the point. Do not get lost in the weeds or labor over every detail. This is not research in the typical sense in that it involves long hours and laborious effort. Simply find the median price range, look for the appropriate zip codes, and focus like a laser beam on those zip codes.

Before we move on I need to make something very clear: You can only sell homes people want to buy. This is a simple yet extremely important concept. It is so important that I suggest you write in on a Post-It and stick it on your computer monitor. This is the all-guiding principle when it comes to flipping real estate deals. You need to have something that people actually want to buy. You will be tempted at times to go after outlier properties. Don't. They take too much time to sell.

When you have homes people want to buy, you will do deals … fast. How fast? Expect to flip homes within two to four weeks, tops. If it takes you longer than that, something is wrong. You might not be in the right zip codes or you may have stepped outside the median price range. Two to four weeks is totally doable but only if you are dealing with the "popular crowd" of nice homes in nice neighborhoods.

Attention! Trulia Heatmap Update.

Due to recent changes in Trulia heat maps, I did a video explaining how to do market research without Trulia heat maps. Go to WholesalingLeaseOptions.com/research to see the video.

3. MARKETING - ONLINE

Now it is time for you, the big fish, to make waves in your small ponds (those zip codes). You will do this via online marketing. The first step is to go to Craigslist and Zillow, and look for listings that are "for rent" or "for sale by owner".

I am not talking about posting ads on these sites. I am talking about contacting the landlords and the sellers of these homes.

Once you have an email or a phone number, it is time to make contact. Personally, I like to send texts, emails, and voicemails — but it is not me who does the sending. I have a VA (virtual assistant) who reaches out on my behalf. When you first start out, you can do this yourself so you get more familiar with the process but the questions remain the same. I use these questions to this day, and they are very simple:

- Is the house still available?
- Are you the owner?
- Would you consider leasing the house for a year and then selling it?

These serve as your screening questions, and any viable prospect should answer "yes" to all three. My VA forwards me a lead only if that person says yes to all three questions. This saves me a ton of time.

This strategy is not very complicated. If you do the work, you will get qualified leads and know that you are heading in the right direction. Do the work and you will see results.

4. MARKETING - OFFLINE

PUT UP BANDIT SIGNS

Ah, bandit signs. Now you will finally know what these are. Chances are you have driven around somewhere in the suburbs and seen signs posted on telephone poles and intersections with handwritten messages that say something to the effect of "We Buy Houses". These are called bandit signs. If you have seen any of these, you may have thought to yourself, "Do those signs really work?" and I can tell you that they absolutely work.

My favorite tactic with bandit signs is to hand write the text (use a thick marker!) and write "I Buy Houses Regardless of Equity - PHONE #". That's it. No website URL, no social media profiles, and no email address. Just the phrase and a phone number.

In my Wholesaling Lease Options course we have an entire module dedicated to bandit signs that my students have shared. Some of the examples are shocking in how simple yet powerful they are. Make sure you are following local ordinances in placing your signs.

The point is that you are now advertising yourself as an investor, and starting to make waves. When people respond to your bandit sign, simply ask them these questions to see if they are a quality lead.

- What's your situation?
- Tell me about your house?
- What would you like to see happen?
- If I can make that happen, how quickly do you need to sell?

- You wouldn't consider leasing your house for a year and then selling it, would you?

The simple action of creating and posting signs creates momentum. Everyone loves momentum, but most people forget that momentum starts with movement. In this case, you are the only one who can make the first splash that turns into waves. I hope that you will be among the to 1% of people who actually take action because if you do, you will experience results that the other 99% of people out there only dream about.

DIRECT MAIL

I want to share one additional marketing strategy: direct mail. You may or may not be ready for direct mail right now, but I mention this so you can refer back to this section when you feel the time is right. Once you add direct mail to your advertising efforts, you will have a three-pronged approach to finding sellers online, on the street, and directly via their mailbox.

Direct mail simply refers to sending mail to lists of people. More specifically, you are going to target 1) absentee owners and 2) homeowners that bought using FHA or VA financing in the last three to seven years. (FHA or VA financing refers to loans insured by the Federal Housing Administration or the Department of Veterans Affairs that did not require hardly any down payments.)

FHA and VA lists are the best to use because of how on-target they are. (And nobody else's marketing to them!) The reason they are so on-target is because of moving times: on average, the typical person today tends to move every five years. This is a change from 2006-2007, when the housing market was booming. In those days, the average homeowner stayed in their house for about three years.

Knowing this, you can cross-reference your zip codes with homeowners who purchased in those zip codes using FHA or VA financing.

These lists contain valuable leads because they are full of people who bought properties with little to no money down. A buyer who used a VA loan put no money down, and an FHA buyer typically put 3% to 3.5% money down. There is a lot of opportunity in these lists because, simply put, you have sellers who want to sell but maybe can't, or don't have enough equity. And most of them can't afford two house payments once they do move.

One final type of mailing list is that of absentee owners. When I talk about mailing to absentee owners, many regular wholesalers disagree with me and cite "too much competition". They believe that many real estate investors are wholesaling and mailing to those people and that throwing your hat into the ring of an already crowded market is foolish.

Here is why they are wrong. You are in a different position because you will be doing lease options, which means you will be focusing on the best zip codes. Real estate investors are sending direct mail to rental zip codes because that is where most of the wholesaling activity is happening. These investors are buying cheap properties and selling them to landlords, which means they are not sending direct mail to nicer, more expensive zip codes.

This is why it is important to focus on homes that people actually want to buy, and if you target absentee owners in those markets you will see a lot less competition.

ZILLOW DIRECT MAIL

The final strategy for direct mail that I am going to show you here leverages the power of Zillow. Let's go back to our Shelby County example and pick the 38016 zip code. Type that zip code into Zillow and change your settings to show only houses. Rental houses are alright, too. Let's say fourteen results show up and all of them look like nice houses in a good part of town.

Simply send a letter to each of these homeowners and repeat the process of finding new properties on Zillow every day. If you have a virtual assistant, this is even easier. Your VA would go into Zillow every day, search 38016, and sort them out. Then you make contact with those homeowners via direct mail. I often use a piece of paper from a yellow legal pad. Yes, it is that simple.

It is important to note that you are not sending these letters to the listed homes, you are sending them to their homeowners. To obtain homeowner addresses, simply go into the county records. You will quickly discover that many of these homeowners are trying to sell but can't — thus they post their property for rent instead. This is perfect because it opens the door for you to come in with lease options. And guess what? Most of these houses are vacant!

Please do not mention "lease options" in your direct mail when contacting these homeowners. Most homeowners do not know what lease options are and you do not want to confuse them. Simply send a letter and say, *"Hey, if you want to sell your house, I want to buy it. Regardless of equity, I will still buy it."*

I use this tactic to this day. Keep it simple and straight to the point. Steer clear of anything complicated or fancy-looking. I can tell you from personal experience that I have seen better results with the simple stuff. I have tried to type up professional looking letters with my logo in the letterhead and an explanation of lease options. It just does not work.

You will face a real temptation to make things more complicated than they need to be. You might be thinking, *"Is this really all you need to do to find a seller?"* The answer is yes, this is really all you need to do.

Let's review what we've talked about in this first chapter.

1. Market Research. First, you are going to do some market research by finding the median price range of homes in a particularly county, and stay within that range. Make sure to stay in markets where the median is above $100,000.

2. Pinpoint Key Zip Codes. Second, you are going to find and catalog the best zip codes according to the market research you did in step one.

3. Marketing - Online. Third, you will start making waves by doing some online marketing. Use sites like Craigslist and Zillow to find qualified leads by sending texts, emails, or voicemails to people asking them *"Is the house still available? Are you the owner? Would you consider leasing the house for a year and then selling it?"*

4. Marketing - Offline. Fourth, you'll put up some bandit signs in the area. Make sure the bandit signs are handwritten with short messages and just a phone number to contact you. Fifth, start sending simple direct mail, yellow letters, to as many FHA/VA home owners and tired landlords as you can.

Remember, success is sequential not simultaneous. If you do these things step-by-step as I have described, you will get qualified leads and be well on your way to flipping your first two deals.

I have worked with hundreds of students over the years, and the first 1-2 deals are the most important because they give you confidence to move forward. The cash in your pocket is also a big plus and that is why I am so adamant about doing these steps in the right order. I want you to make those first two deals … quickly. As I said earlier in this chapter, you should expect to close deals within 45-60 days tops if you are doing everything correctly.

You might be reading this and think that 1-2 months is not quick enough because you need cash flow right away. I completely understand. I have been in that situation, as I shared in the introduction to this book. If that is you then skip ahead to the last chapter to find out about an opportunity to speed up the process.

In the next chapter, we will be talking about making the offer. This is the second major part of Wholesaling Lease Options, and frankly I think it is more exciting than the stuff we have covered so far. Why? Because it is a big step towards closing your first deal.

Are you ready? Then join me in Chapter 2 and you will learn the surprising truth about making an offer for Wholesaling Lease Options deals.

2
MAKING THE OFFER

"You don't have to be great to start, but you have to start to be great."

— Zig Ziglar

What comes to mind when you think of "sales"? If you are like most people, the idea of "sales" feels a bit icky. Maybe the image of a pushy real estate agent comes to mind, or a slimy used car salesman. But I propose that if you've ever persuaded or convinced anyone of anything, you are already in the business of sales. (By the way, one of the best deals I ever closed was convincing my wife to marry me! So I am a HUGE fan of sales.)

Automation is going to be key in taking the heavy load of sales off your shoulders. However, the more you know about sales the better. To reframe this concept a bit, I encourage you to think not of sales, but of simply making an offer.

With Wholesaling Lease Options, you're simply *making an offer* to someone who happens to be selling his or her home. The strategies you learn in this chapter will be among the most profitable you'll ever learn, not just for your business but for your life.

Remember, this is still your "Average Joe" speaking to you. I'm not some sales expert guru kind of guy. I don't have any smooth-talking sales scripts, or play any weird sales "mind game". All that can seem cool, but when it comes to flipping deals, you just have to take action.

If complexity is the enemy of execution, then simplicity is the key to taking action. To reiterate the Zig Ziglar quote above, *"You don't have to be great to start, but you have to start to be great."* Let's get started.

BE THE RELUCTANT BUYER

First, there are only two types of people you will deal with: someone who is "in" and someone who is "out" - someone who is motivated and someone who is not. A seller is either a "suspect" or a "prospect". Quite simply, a "prospect" is someone who wants to sell their home, and a "suspect" is someone who has zero interest in selling their home. You only want to spend your time with prospects.

It is important to understand that you can only do deals with motivated sellers. So if they are not motivated, that is okay. Move on... Make an offer and move on to the next seller. You are only looking for motivated sellers. And they are out there... Don't ever forget that. You have to find them, and that may take some time... But they are out there.

You are not looking for someone who just "wants" to sell their home. You are looking for someone that "needs" to sell their home. Do you understand the difference?

While you are looking for motivated sellers, you want to make sure you are not becoming the motivated buyer. You need to be the "Reluctant Buyer".

Being the "Reluctant Buyer" means that you are looking for motivated sellers that have a problem you can solve, sellers that need to sell their house.

The Seller should be selling you on their home. The Seller should be trying to convince you why you should make an offer on their home. They're the one with the problem - not you!

Do you see the difference? You are not selling a "Lease Option Program". You're just making an offer on their property. They can either take it or leave it. It is no big deal.

The main point I am trying to make is to not be so wrapped up in the outcome. Don't feel like you have to be a really good, super aggressive, high-pressure salesman.

In fact, the more you are like that, the less likely you are to do a lot of deals. One of the things I learned early on was, *"The harder you chase a seller, the faster they'll run."*

When you are the "Reluctant Buyer" and they are the "Motivated Seller" - then you have a pretty sweet deal on your hands - and everyone wins.

Sometimes I like to ask this question to sellers, "Mr Seller, thanks for calling me back. Do you mind if I ask you a few questions about your house to see if it would even be something I would be interested in?"

So it is important that you don't beg someone to sell their house to you, or try to talk them into it. And don't offer up some long-winded explanation of what a Lease Options is, either — it is just not necessary. Don't overcomplicate things.

They are either in or they're out. You can help them, or you can't. It is a "Yes" or a "No". They need to make a decision now or never. They need to "sh*t or get off the pot" - as one of my mentors taught me.

Remove yourself from the outcome. Get to the "No" as quickly as possible. Just ask questions, make an offer, and move on to the next lead. (And or course, follow-up. More on that later.)

QUESTIONS TO ASK SELLERS WHEN MAKING INITIAL CONTACT

When being the Reluctant Buyer, I sometimes like to use "negative phrasing". These initial questions /

statements can really set the tone in a way that opens up further conversation. I'm not exactly sure why, and I'm sure some sales psychologist guru out there could explain it, but for our purposes here, you just need to know that these phrases work when starting a conversation with a seller:

- *"Did I catch you at a bad time?"*
- *"It sounds like you're busy?"*
- *"It sounds like I caught you in the middle of something."*

These phrases work extremely well, possibly because the person's response is almost always positive. The conversation usually goes this way:

Me: *"Hi Dave, it's Joe. Did I catch you at a bad time?"*
Dave: *"Oh no, no, this is fine. I can talk…"*

Personally, I've often responded the same way when friends call. Just today as I'm writing this, a good friend called and said, *"You wouldn't have just a minute or two, would you?"* (Notice the negative phrasing?) I was actually very busy, but I ended up instinctively saying, *"Yes I do."* This stuff works.

Once the seller responds, and invites me in, as it were, I say something like, *"So, I got your text / voicemail and I am calling you back."*

Or if you're not actually "calling them back", you could say something like, *"Hi! I saw your house on Zillow. I am an investor and I am looking for a nice house in a nice neighborhood. Can you tell me a little bit about your house? Is it a nice home?"*

Or, you could say, *"Do you mind if I ask you a few questions about your house? I'm an investor and would like to see if it would be something I'm interested in."*

The main thing I am trying to do here is to make the homeowner sell their house to me, instead of the other way around. This is a million-dollar tip! It is a complete game changer in closing deals.

Start asking questions about their situation…

"So tell me… What's your situation?"

"What would you like to see happen?"

"If I can make that happen, how soon do you need to sell this house? Why that time frame?"

Did you notice that I am not really asking questions about the property? I am trying to dig more into WHY they need to sell it - or not.

It is also important that you push the "pain" button a bit and dig into why they haven't sold their house yet. This might make you a bit uncomfortable but it is an important step to finding out if this person is a candidate for lease options.

Here are some other questions to ask:

"Sounds like a really nice house! Why hasn't it sold yet?"

"I don't get it, it looks like a really nice house. Why would you even want to sell it?"

"It sounds like you really want to sell the house quickly. And it looks like a pretty sweet deal. But I am not sure I can actually help you. I don't think you need me. Why don't you just list it with a Realtor?"

"So how long has the Realtor had it listed? I'm sure you've been getting tons of showings and offers, right?"

"What are you going to do if you can't sell the house? Are you going to rent it?" (Boom… Value Bomb Right There… That's my favorite question…)

If they say yes to this last question, then you've just found a perfect lease option candidate. Why? Because the owner wants to sell, but can't, and probably doesn't want to be a landlord. You are saving the seller from having to be a landlord by offering a solution to their predicament - a lease option.

Once the seller confirms they might have to rent, ask them…

"Well, if you rent your house would you rather rent it to somebody who is going to call you every time the faucet leaks or would you rather rent to somebody who wants to buy it? Someone who is going to take care of the home and actually fix the faucet themselves — without calling you?"

Big difference, right? This type of question gets the seller thinking.

Then follow-up with, *"Hey, you know what? I'm looking for a rental property that I can rent for maybe a year or two and then buy. That wouldn't work for you, would it?"* (Notice the negative phrasing again?)

The seller hopefully realizes by now that you are looking for an investment property and not for your own next residence. They also know you are an investor who only wants to rent / buy nice homes in nice areas. All of this reframes the conversation. The deal has to also work for you, the investor.

This is the best approach I've learned from years of flipping deals. I've tried much more complicated strategies in the past. I used to focus primarily on building a bunch of rapport and pitching all the benefits of lease options (even if the seller wasn't interested). This is a recipe for wasting tons of time.

To help you understand the big picture of what we're doing, instead of talking on and on about all the benefits of doing a Lease Option with me, I've turned the "selling" into simple questions. Like this:

"I don't know if this will actually work for you, but what if I could lease the property from you for a year or two, take care of all the normal maintenance and repairs, pay the rent on-time every month, whether it is vacant or not, and then buy the house from you at the end without you having to pay any real estate commissions... What would you want to do then?"

This approach puts the ball back into the seller's court by giving them a simple "what if" to consider. Again, simplicity is the key here. There are more in-depth questions I teach in my Wholesaling Lease Options course, but this first batch of questions can definitely get you started.

PROSPECTS OR SUSPECTS

I have a simple rule when dealing with sellers. A seller is either a "prospect" or a "suspect".

If they are interested in doing a Lease Option, and there is some motivation, they are a "prospect". I will make them an offer on the phone (actually by Skype or Zoom if possible, so I can see them and they can see me). If the house is close enough to me, I will make an appointment to go see the house and meet with them in person.

If they are not motivated yet, or they aren't interested in a Lease Option, they are a "suspect". And

I am just going to send them an offer - by mail and email.

Make appointments with prospects. Make offers to suspects.

THE 3 TYPES OF OFFERS

When it is time to send an offer, I send three different types of offer: the cash offer, the Sandwich Lease Options offer, and the Wholesaling Lease Options offer. These three options are part of my credibility kit, which you can create with a few clicks of my Lease Options Software. I demonstrate the Lease Options Software in my full-length masterclass (WLOwebinar.com).

Why do I send multiple option offers? Because typically I want to just start a conversation and get my foot in the door. I want to give the seller options. Something your competition is not doing, by the way.

OFFER #1. THE CASH OFFER

The first option is a cash offer. You can calculate the cash offer by using the standard MAO (Maximum Allowable Offer) formula which is:

Maximum Allowable Offer = After Repair Value x 70% - Repairs - Wholesale Fee

First, find the After Repair Value or ARV of the house. You can find the ARV online from real estate sites like Zillow, Eppraisal, RealQuest, iComps, or Redfin.

You can grab the first ARV you see online or take the average ARV from multiple sites. Continue using the formula and multiple the ARV by 70%, subtract repairs, and subtract your fee.

How do you know what to subtract for repairs? Let me give you an example. In St. Louis where I live, repairs often fall within the $5 to $20 per square foot range. Even if the seller says the property doesn't need any work, you should still subtract something for repairs. In this case, I might go with $5 per square foot.

If the seller says the property could use some minor cosmetic work like paint and carpet repairs, subtract $10 per square foot. If the property needs more than that, go with the $15 or $20 per square foot.

To make this even less work for myself, my VA calculates the offers for me, and sends them to the seller, all using my simple Lease Options Software.

The key to this is to not complicate it or over think it. Just make an offer as quickly as you can. If the seller accepts your letter of intent, then you can dig more into the numbers (ex. review your repair estimate and comps in more detail) to make sure your offer is semi-accurate.

Figuring out your fee is entirely up to you. My advice is that you should be trying to make at least $10,000 on each cash deal. This is what I shoot for on my wholesale deals. Granted there are times when my fee varies, but this is a good place to start.

You might be thrown off by reading about "cash offers" here. Aren't we doing lease options? Yes, and there is a method to the madness. The cash offer anchors the lease option offer by presenting a lowball number. Your cash offer will be cheap in the eyes of the seller and they very well may think it is ridiculous. This is perfectly fine. You're making this cash offer so that your lease option offer looks so much better by comparison.

OFFER #2. THE SANDWICH LEASE OPTION OFFER

The second offer is called the Sandwich Lease Option, which I like to call my "Perfect Tenant Program." This offer is called that because I am the perfect tenant. I will be staying in the middle of the deal, taking care of the maintenance and vacancies. In this situation, you will make the most money because you will be staying in the middle. You'll get cash now, cash flow, and cash later.

When you do this, you should be making about $30,000-$50,000 on each Sandwich Lease Option deal. Don't worry, the seller wins on this deal as well because you are offering close to the same equity they would get if they sold with a Realtor. The option price is calculated by taking the ARV, and multiplying it by 85% — which is on average how much they would walk away with if they sold with a Realtor, and by factoring in discounts, repairs, carrying costs, closing costs, etc.

The next step involves rent. You should propose a 25% discount off the market rent with a lease term of at least 3 to 5 years. When you present this "perfect tenant offer" you are basically saying: "Look, I'm an investor. I'm going to put somebody in your house as a tenant-buyer and I will manage the property from beginning to end. You don't have to worry about anything. In return, I get a little bit of the equity and some of the cash flow."

There are really only two possible outcomes when making this offer. The seller may agree to what you have offered or the seller may reject the offer on the grounds that your terms don't work for them. Sometimes the seller wants a larger down payment or wants to stay more in control of the property. Perhaps the seller is just not super motivated yet.

Whatever the seller's reasons, a rejection is not the end of the road. Instead, it opens the door for a lease option assignment which is the third and final option in our offer to the seller.

OFFER #3. THE LEASE OPTION ASSIGNMENT OR WHOLESALING LEASE OPTION OFFER

The lease option assignment is just another way of saying Wholesaling Lease Option — which we do by getting a lease option contract and assigning it to a tenant-buyer. This is different than regular wholesaling where you assign the contract to an investor. With a Wholesaling Lease Options deal, you wholesale the lease option contract to a tenant-buyer. Hopefully, the difference is clear to you. It is important to understand the difference between regular wholesaling and Wholesaling Lease Options.

Now, what is our lease option price? In this case, the option price will be whatever the seller wants. The rents will be whatever the market rents are. And the terms will often be one to two years. Remember what I said earlier: you want to make at least $5,000 on these deals so that is what you will set as your assignment fee.

If this doesn't make any sense to you, watch my in-depth training in this free video masterclass (www.WLOwebinar.com) where I go thru some more case studies and examples.

When it is all put together, a Wholesale Lease Option is very simple:

- First, you get the property under contract with a seller. You are the tenant-buyer.

- Second, you turn around and advertise that contract.

- Third, you sell the contract to someone for an assignment fee.

To help this sink in, let's go back (yet again) to our Shelby County example and look at the three options in our offer to the seller.

First, let's put together the cash offer. Look up the ARV estimate which you can grab off Zillow (they refer to this as their "Zestimate", a little play on their branding). For a typical Shelby County house in our targeted zip codes, let's say the ARV estimate is $163,101. For our cash offer, we want a 70% discount off the ARV.

Next, we look at the square footage of the house which is say 2,500 sq. feet. We can tell from the pictures on the site that the property doesn't need repairs, so we put $0 for repairs. Finally, it is time to consider our fee as wholesalers. We want to make about $10,000.

Putting all those pieces together, we therefore make a cash offer of $104,171 ($163,101 x 70% - (2500 x $0) - $10,000). It is not likely the seller will accept this offer. They're more likely to want to sell close to the price listed on Zillow, so let's say they want $160,000. That is just $3,101 less than Zillow's Zestimate for the place.

How do we respond? With questions. First, we want to find out what they think the house will rent for. Second, we want to find out how much they need to sell it for. Third, we need to find out what how much money they need to walk away with from any deal we agree on.

I then send a voice memo to my VA to put these numbers into a spreadsheet. The spreadsheet auto-calculates the totals for our offers. Now, I realize I'm brushing over a lot of the math but that is because you don't need to spend time doing it. The spreadsheet does the calculations for the VA.

Below is an example of the spreadsheet. I have recently stopped using the spreadsheet since my Lease Options Software does all this now:

As you can see in the spreadsheet, the first offer which is the cash offer is $104,171. The second offer, the Sandwich Lease Option, comes out to $138,636. The third offer, the lease option, comes in at about $160,000.

Together, these offers give the seller three totals to consider: $104,171, $138,636, and $160,000. The variety of offers changes the conversation from a flat "yes" or "no" to an ongoing dialogue about "which one". To be clear, I always make three offers and all three go into my credibility kit, which we will discuss next.

THE CREDIBILITY KIT

The credibility kit is a package of materials that clearly and immediately conveys professionalism to the sellers you approach. Your credibility kit includes five items:

1. A cover letter
2. A letter of intent (where you list your three offers)
3. An explanation of what a lease option is and a summary of the benefits
4. A frequently asked questions (FAQ) list
5. A page of references

Additionally, there are two other ways to boost credibility with sellers and I recommend these to all of my students. The first is a membership with the Better Business Bureau, or the BBB for short. You've probably heard of the BBB and may even think the BBB itself is a rip-off, but it does wonders for boosting your credibility. The BBB fees vary by location but for my area, it costs about $450 for a year. The second thing I recommend is to join your local Chamber of Commerce. These are simple and powerful ways to boost your authority. I will show you how to incorporate these into your credibility kit.

THE COVER LETTER

Your cover letter should not be some long, drawn out document. In effect, most of my cover letters simply say, *"Hey, it was nice talking to you. Please review the different lease purchase offers."* Here is an example of one of my cover letters:

---

generic logo company

Joe's Property Holdings, LLC
2978 Laguna Hills Trail
San Diego CA 98769
619-987-0976

<<Date>>

<<Seller Name>>
<<Mailing Street Address>>
<<Mailing City, State Zip>>

Dear <<Seller Name>>,

It was nice talking with you today about your house at <<Property Street Address>>. I understand that now may not be a good time to sell your house to us. But if circumstances change, we'd love to talk with you again.

Please review the attached options we can offer to buy your house, and keep this letter for future reference.

Remember, we can ***buy your house "as-is", for a fair price, on any date you choose***.

Sincerely,

[signature]

(note: for a quick signature font, see http://www.mylivesignature.com/)

YOUR NAME
YOUR PHONE
WEBSITE?

A short letter aligns with your initial contact with the seller (short letters, brief text messages, and so forth) and it also saves you time.

You're probably picking up my preference for speed and simplicity. In fact, if there is ever a time when I'm on the phone with a seller I often pretend like I'm in a hurry to keep the call short. Once I gather the necessary information, I prep the seller for my credibility kit by saying, *"I'm going to send you some information. Look it over and let's talk about it."*

THE LETTER OF INTENT

Here is a screenshot of my letter of intent. You will see the three offers: the Cash, Sandwich Lease, and Lease Options Assignment:

LETTER OF INTENT - MULTIPLE OPTIONS

Date: _____

Property Address: _____

Thank you for the opportunity to review and consider your home. We can buy your home any of the following ways, and close through a real estate attorney or title company within seven business days.

OPTION 1 - Cash
- Purchase Price: **$238,929**
- Close in 7-30 Days
- Buyer to pay all closing costs

OPTION 2 – Sandwich Lease Option - *"Perfect Tenant Program"*
- Option Price: **$420,243**
- Option Consideration: $1,000
- Monthly Rent: $1,950
- Term: Minimum 5 Years
- *Note: We are the tenant-buyer, but we will sub-lease the house to another tenant-buyer. We will stay in the middle for the entire term, pay the rent every month even if the house is vacant, and be responsible for all the regular maintenance and repairs under $500.*

OPTION 3 – Lease Option Assignment
- Option Price: **$485,000**
- Option Consideration: $1,000
- Monthly Rent: $2,600
- Term: Minimum 2 Years
- *Note: If we can't do Option #2 and stay in the middle, we will assign our Lease Option to a pre-qualified tenant-buyer, only with your written authorization.*

OPTION 4 - Lease Option Consulting
- If you would like to learn how to do a Lease Option yourself, we can consult with you and teach you how to do them. Our consulting fee is one month's rent, paid in advance.

OTHER POSSIBILITIES – LET'S TALK!

Call me if you have any questions @ 555-555-5555.

NOTE: If your property is listed with an agent, please give this Letter of Intent to your Realtor and have them contact us.

Option That Most Interests You: _____

Seller(s) Acceptance: _____ Date: _____

Look closely and you'll see there is a fourth option that I offer at the bottom: Lease Option Consulting. Consulting is one of the coolest things I teach in my Wholesaling Lease Options course. The consulting option goes beyond the scope of this book, but in short, consulting is a great option because you've already positioned yourself as an investor.

A seller may not want to do a Sandwich Lease Option because the money may not be enough. A seller may not want to do the lease option assignment either because he or she doesn't want you to keep all the option deposit money.

The consulting option says, *"Maybe I can teach you on how to do the lease option yourself."* As a consultant you could charge the seller a minimum fee of one month's rent or whatever you work out (I often tell students that $2,500 is a good place to start). This would equate to two to four hours of consulting.

After listing the offers, you should summarize the benefits in a way that describes how a lease option program works. Here is an example of my benefits summary sheet:

Why is a LEASE OPTION Becoming a Top Choice Alternative to Selling a Home?

Our fast, easy approach to home selling has helped hundreds of people in the United States. How can it help you?

Our objective is to make this as SIMPLE AS POSSIBLE for you so that you can move on with your life, and quit worrying about your house.

It is our goal to ensure the process of selling your home is a smooth and easy one for you. We strive to achieve a win-win-win situation in all our lease option purchases.

You, as the seller of the house, win by receiving the assurance of knowing that while the house is being sold, all of the expenses are taken care of, the house is maintained, and you are receiving all of the tax benefits associated with being a landlord, with none of the management responsibilities.

Our tenant/buyer wins by getting to own a home in a shorter amount of time than it would take them if they were trying to buy conventionally, as well as being able to immediately occupy their new home, while qualifying for a loan. We have created a system that creates the paperwork that mortgage lenders look for when qualifying people for loans to assist our tenant/buyers. In addition, we give our tenant/buyers immediate credit tips to assist in the loan qualification process.

We win by profiting from the sale of the home, as well as gaining two more satisfied customers. The reason that we are in business, of course, is to make a profit, as well as to use our expertise in real estate transactions to assist homebuyers and sellers in making the sale or purchase of their home an easy, stress-free one.

Summary of Benefits For You:

- No more vacancies
- We take the house in an as-is condition
- Save or repair your credit
- Immediate debt relief
- We make your payments, guaranteed.
- No more missed or late mortgage payments
- No management / rental headaches.
- No more minor repairs
- Opportunity for significant increase in total income
- You retain all property tax benefits
- You may qualify for additional tax deductions (including depreciation, improvements, and repairs)

THE FAQ SHEET

The FAQ is simply another document that answers many of the basic questions a seller may have. A strong FAQ page serves as an "objection crusher" and adds an incredible amount of authority to your offer. Here is an example:

Frequently Asked Questions...

What is a Lease Option?

A lease option is essentially a purchase contract combined with a rental agreement. The buyer leases the property for a specified period of time and then has the option of purchasing the property before the end of the lease agreement. Sales price, length of rental, closing costs, and maintenance are all negotiated much the same as a conventional real estate transaction. A lease option, if properly utilized, is both a seller and a buyer's dream come true because it can eliminate many of the negatives normally attributed to the selling and buying of a home.

How does it work?

We present a monthly lease amount as well as a pre-determined sales price that is agreed to by all parties. A lease option / purchase is basically a monthly lease set up over a pre-determined period of time. At the end of that time, we purchase the home from you for whatever the pre-determined price is.

The basics are simple:
- You rent your property to COMPANY, LLC
- You give COMPANY, LLC the right to buy your property for a set price.
- COMPANY, LLC places a tenant/buyer in your property.
- The tenant/buyer receives the right to buy your property at or above your agreed

As you would expect, we have all of these templates available inside my Wholesaling Lease Options course.

#4. REFERENCES

You might be wondering what to list for references, especially if you're just starting out. For starters, this is where you would mention your membership in the Better Business Bureau and the Chamber of Commerce. Students in my Wholesaling Lease Options course have the option of using the name of my attorney as a reference. I also have a nationwide mortgage broker and tenant screening company who students can list if they are part of my program.

The bottom line is that only you know your references. Think about any realtors, insurance agents, or property management companies you know. It also doesn't hurt to put a personal reference from another investor. I often allow my best students to use me as a personal reference. Having these references will crush any sense in the seller's mind that you're some "fly by night" scam.

SENDING THE CREDIBILITY KIT

When you have all these components ready, your credibility kit is ready to ship. You can send your kit via email, but I prefer to send it via physical mail because it creates much more authority.

If you think going to the post office is going to eat up a ton of your time, you would be right! This is why I recommend using a VA. My VA is in the Philippines uses the magic of the internet to go to a website, print out my credibility kit with the seller's name and address, and ship the package from a U.S. return address. Are you beginning to see how easy this can be?

THE FORTUNE IS IN THE FOLLOW-UP

Your work isn't over yet. Once the credibility kit is shipped, you must follow-up. Follow-up is a must because most sellers are going to say "no" to start. I recommend following up every single month with every single seller you have targeted. Remember that some of these properties will end up sitting on the market for months. Sellers will get increasingly anxious about carrying costs and may be more open to doing a deal.

If following up once a month sounds like a lot of work, it is not — if you have a VA. Each month, your VA could send a text to each of your sellers with something short like, *"Hey, have you sold your house yet?"* Or your VA can send a postcard to sellers with a note that says, *"Hey, I'm surprised I haven't heard back from you. I'm still very interested in buying your house. Please call me, thanks."* You can even send a broadcast voicemail that says, *"Hey it's Joe. You probably don't remember me but we talked a little while ago about your house… etc"*

This VA stuff can seem overwhelming which is why I offer VA training for students of my Wholesaling Lease Options course to give to their VA. VA setup is outside the scope of this book, but I mention it here because I want you to be aware of what is possible.

You must be diligent on the follow-up. Approximately 50% of deals happen because of the follow-up!

Everything I've described so far is a no-pressure way to make deals. If you send the kit and it leads to a deal, great! If it doesn't work, you move onto the next one. Either way, it is no big deal. It is not like you have spent loads of time doing research, crunching numbers, or talking to a seller on the phone. Research, market, and automate.

START TO BE GREAT

Remember the quote I shared at the start of this chapter by Zig Ziglar: *"You don't have to be great to start, but you have to start to be great."* If you follow these steps, you will see success. There is simply too much real estate and too many buyers and sellers for you to ever run out of opportunities.

If you're ready to jump right into Wholesaling Lease Options, make sure to carve out some time and check out www.WLOwebinar.com. You'll get more in-depth training in this video masterclass, absolutely free. You will also get information on my course, Wholesaling Lease Options, to see if it is a fit for you.

In the next chapter, we are going to talk about finding the tenant-buyer. The tenant-buyer is a key player in Wholesaling Lease Options. I'm going to show you how to find a good one and how to avoid a situation where you get stuck holding a property without a tenant-buyer. Let's go to the next chapter.

3

FINDING THE TENANT-BUYER

"Never say more than is necessary."

— Richard Brinsley Sheridan

The tenant-buyer is crucial for obvious reasons: this is the person who will occupy the home and ultimately buy the lease option contract from you. We are going to have to do a little math in this section, but don't be intimidated. It is important to understand this so that you learn how to make the numbers work for you.

Let's go back to our Shelby County example from the previous chapters. Say you have sent your credibility kit to the seller and your offer was accepted. Before you turn our attention to finding a tenant-buyer, the first thing you need to do is mark the price up a little bit to cover your assignment fee and any rent credits.

NON-EXCLUSIVE OPTION AND CONTINGENCIES

This is very important to understand. At no time during this initial lease option period are we ever responsible for paying the rent. Our agreement with the seller is non-exclusive. So we are not "tying up" the property. If the seller rents or sells the house before we do, they can cancel our agreement and they won't owe us anything.

In my Wholesaling Lease Option agreements, my initial option contract is contingent on two things: 1) my inspection of the property, and 2) me and the seller completing a more formal Lease Option Agreement. I can't go into much detail here, but the deal is not complete until I do both of those things. And I am not going to complete a more formal Lease Option Agreement until I find a qualified tenant-buyer to assign my contract to. The seller knows all of this upfront. Nothing is being hidden from the seller.

This is the wonderful thing about options. All we have is an option to buy the property. It is the ultimate "control without ownership". We are removed from virtually all liability. We have very little at risk on these deals.

LOOKING AT COMPS

Now we need to look more carefully at the comparables of the property. You will get good comps by first looking at what price the seller is looking to walk away with. In our example, the seller wants $160,000 and $1,650 a month in rent. If we cross-reference this property with Zillow's Zestimate, we find that Zillow says it's worth about $163,000.

A quick note on looking for comps online... I've mentioned Zillow a lot but there are others you can utilize as well. Checking the comps on these other sites can give you a well-rounded estimate on the value of the home. Some other sites are:

- Redfin.com
- Realtor.com
- Eppraisal.com
- RealQuestExpress.com
- iComps.com

For this property, Realtor.com thinks the property is worth $161,000, iComps.com estimates the value at $158,000, and eppraisal.com has a pretty high opinion of the place at $170,000. Seeing these four values puts us in a better position to think about the seller's offer and the numbers are all within the same ballpark. This is a good sign.

I also like to look at sold comps on Redfin.

SETTING THE ASSIGNMENT FEE

Generally, I ballpark about 3% of the sellers price for my assignment fee. Or, I try to make at least $5,000. On this deal, 3% of $160,000 is $4,800 so I'm just going to round up to $5,000.

If you work with the mortgage broker that I recommend in my course, he can make sure that the tenant-buyer gets this money back as part of their future down payment. (My mortgage broker can do these loans in all 50 States.)

This arrangement can be quite flexible. Let's say the tenant buyer only has $3,000 (instead of the $5,000 for my assignment fee) but can easily afford the payments on the house. If they are good quality tenant-buyers (which means they have a realistic chance of getting a mortgage in 12-24 months), I can take the $3,000 now and set a note for the difference of $2,000 to be taken over the next twenty-four months. If I divide $2,000 by 24, that equals about $83 per month. Now we can set up a payment plan of $83 a month for 24 months. You can even shorten the length of the payment plan to 12 months if the tenant-buyer is agreeable to that.

A little flexibility can go a long way. Do this on all your deals, and you'll be able to snag some good passive income.

HOW TO SET THE RENT

Now it is time to think about the rent. Remember, the seller wants $1,650/mo. Once again, we will get an idea of the market value by looking at a few websites - Zillow and Rentometer. Zillow estimates the rent to be around $1,425 per month. Compared to $1,650 that is a bit of a gap - which is worth looking into. If there is a gap like this, it's important to look at similar properties on Zillow to see what their rents are.

You can also cross-reference rents on Rentometer.com. You should be fine with just the free version which gives you about three reviews. The free version is enough and keeps things simple. Rentometer considers the average rent for houses nearby to be just $1,200 per month.

Why such a big gap? Well, the seller may just be asking too much. Or, maybe this house is just nicer than the others in the area. We need to do some more research. We may find some other properties with higher rents.

If we go to Zillow, we can eyeball the photos and square footage to see what other properties similar to this one are listed for. In this Shelby County example, I found a comparable home on Zillow that was renting for $1,795 and another for $1,600. That is more in-line with what we're targeting.

If there was a large discrepancy between what the seller wanted and what similar homes are renting for, you might be wondering how we're going to handle that. No worries, there's a cool thing we can do here with my Wholesaling Lease Options strategy.

If the seller's rent is too high, we can advertise the property at that amount and see if we get any takers. If we don't find a good tenant-buyer in 2-3 weeks, then it's no big deal -- we can always go back to the seller and negotiate a lower rent - or just cancel our contract. A conversation like this is possible because we are not obligated to make any rental payments on a lease option flip.

So in this example, we will go ahead and advertise $1,650 in rent.

RENT CREDITS

Sometimes we offer rent credits, sometimes we don't. It just depends.

Rent credits are seller concessions that apply to tenant-buyers closing costs. This money does not go towards their down payment, and it is not money the seller has to set aside every month. To clarify, let's go back to our example. Let's say I list rent credits at $250 per month for twelve months. That comes out to $3,000 per year.

SETTING THE FINAL OPTION PRICE

Now I need to set my option price - the price that I am going to advertise the property. In this case, I am going to set it at $168,000.

How did I get that number? I take the seller's asking price of $160,000 and add the $5,000 that I want to make off the deal (my assignment fee). That gets us to $165,000. And then I add the rent credits of $3,000. That gets us to $168,000.

$160,000 + $5,000 + $3,000 = $168,000

In a nutshell, we give the seller the price they want and mark it up a bit. I get paid from the tenant-buyer. The seller never pays me anything. I mark up their price to cover my assignment fee.

So in summary, this is how I will advertise this property:

- Rent To Own / Lease Option
- Beautiful 3 bedroom home in the Hamilton School District
- Option Price = $168,000
- Option Fee: $5,000
- Rent: $1,650/mo
- Rent Credits: $250/mo for 12 months
- Term: 24 months

Advertising to Find A Good Tenant-Buyer

Now we need to find a tenant-buyer. There are four main ways to advertise this contract / property:

- Craigslist (For Rent and FSBO)
- Zillow (For Rent OR FSBO)
- Signs - in the yard, and in the neighborhood on weekends.
- Facebook Ads

There is a lot I could say about marketing your properties. But it's actually pretty simple. If you do these things and you can't find a good tenant-buyer in 3-4 weeks, then something is really wrong. Either the property is overpriced, or you are not putting it in front of the right people.

GET SOMEONE TO DO ALL THIS FOR YOU

I have talked quite a bit about outsourcing and up to this point the key player in carrying the grunt work has been your VA (Virtual Assistant). We're going to outsource all this marketing as well, but instead of a VA, we're going to find a leasing agent (a Realtor).

When hiring a leasing agent for advertising, I typically offer half of one month's rent as compensation. Most people don't believe me, that I can find a Realtor to market my homes for only half of one month's rent. But whatever... Pay them more if you want. ;)

To find a leasing agent, simply put an ad on Craigslist or contact a leasing agent that you find advertising other properties on Craigslist.

I absolutely recommend finding a leasing agent instead of doing all this yourself. Remember, you are here to flip deals, not run a bunch of ads, take a bunch of calls, and drive around town showing homes.

Just give them the "Selling Homes Checklist" from my Wholesaling Lease Options course.

Once you find an agent and your advertising is rolling, it is time to focus on pre-qualifying the tenant-buyer.

PRE-QUALIFYING THE TENANT-BUYER

Pre-qualifying is obviously important but as you can imagine, I'm going to tell you to outsource this as well. I have an agent and a tenant-screening company who does this for me. Whenever I have a possible tenant-buyer, my agent sends them an application, collects the application fee, and sends the application to my tenant-screening company.

I also have a mortgage broker that I work with who understands lease options

A good tenant-screening company will do everything you would expect: pull their credit history, criminal history, call their references, previous employers, previous landlords, etc. They will also verify each applicant's income.

Here are a some important questions that your mortgage broker should be telling you:

1. Can the applicant afford the home?
2. Do they have at least 3% to 5% to put down?
3. Do they have a realistic chance of getting a mortgage in one to two years?
4. What do they need to do to fix their credit and get a mortgage?

These are very important questions. I say this because of what I have recently heard from one my best students, Adam.

Adam sent me a testimonial recently and said he has done about eight lease option deals and 100% of his tenant-buyers qualified for a mortgage in a year or less. How did Adam do it? By working closely with mortgage brokers like mine, and making sure that the tenant-buyers in each of his deals had a realistic chance of getting a mortgage in one or two years.

My mortgage broker (who is connected to my course) works with people in all fifty states. If you are a member of my Wholesaling Lease Options course, this mortgage broker can help you just like they've helped Adam. If you'd rather find a mortgage broker yourself, though, that's fine too. If so, find somebody that understands lease options.

The bottom line is this: only choose tenant-buyers who have a realistic chance of getting a mortgage and can afford the home.

ASSIGN THE CONTRACT TO THE TENANT-BUYER

Now that you have a good tenant-buyer, it's time to do the rest of the paperwork, collect the option deposit, and assign the contracts.

It is really important that you work with an attorney and/or escrow company in this part of the deal. You want the tenant-buyer to make their option deposit check out to the Escrow Company, not you the investor. This way, it will be easier for the bank to make this money apply to their future down payment.

You also want to make sure there is a 3rd party servicing company that is collecting the rent and paying the mortgage every month. You do not want to be in a situation where the tenant-buyer has been paying the rent, but the seller hasn't been paying the mortgage payment. This is a non-negotiable with me.

At this point you can expect to complete some light paperwork which involves just three documents:

1) a new lease and 2) a new option agreement (both signed by you and the seller), and 3) an assignment agreement. You will assign this paperwork to the tenant-buyer.

Paperwork is where the rubber meets the road. All of it matters and none of it can be overlooked — otherwise you will not get paid and you open yourself to unnecessary risk.

To ensure you have a good handle on everything, I recommend that you crate a rock solid checklist. I have a saying: "checklist leads to checks." You want to make sure that nothing is forgotten or overlooked.

I've given you a bird's-eye view of how Wholesaling Lease Options work, and now it's time to move onto chapter 4.

This will be the most important chapter yet because it will put all the pieces together. You will see how to do your first lease options deal as quickly as possible. You will also get some success principles that I've learned from my experience in the game.

As I've mentioned in previous chapters, I also recommend you carve out some time to dive into my free masterclass at WLOwebinar.com. You'll get more in-depth training in this video masterclass, absolutely free. You'll also get information on my course, Wholesaling Lease Options, to see if it's a fit for you.

4

PUTTING IT ALL TOGETHER (HOW TO MAKE A FULL-TIME INCOME WHOLESALING LEASE OPTIONS)

"Aha!"

"*Aha!*" That's what I think you'll be saying by the end of this chapter. Why? Because like I mentioned back in Chapter 3, this one puts all the pieces together.

Allow me to put on my "Coach Joe" hat and talk for bit about some success principles. Ultimately, this business comes down to you… You are the one that is responsible for your success.

Simply wanting to succeed is not enough — it requires the right mindset, massive action, and rock-solid consistency. Let me share 7 success principles that have been the "glue" that holds everything I do together.

SUCCESS PRINCIPLE #1. KEEP IT SIMPLE

This business is so darn easy to complicate! When you start thinking of all the things to do, keep track of, and manage, you can see how easy it would be to get overwhelmed. When overwhelm sets in, it does more than grow your to-do list, it breeds a ton of "What if" questions. This leads to overthinking and worry. Overthinking is self-defeating and worse — it doesn't help you make any money.

Simplicity, on the other hand, helps you make money. That is true of your first deal and every deal thereafter. If you want to scale to do more deals, you need systems -- but you can't create systems unless you keep it simple. When things get too complicated, you're likely doing something wrong or listening to the wrong teacher. Keep it simple!

SUCCESS PRINCIPLE #2. MODEL WHAT WORKS

Take this from me: this is not the kind of business where you want to reinvent the wheel. Reinventing the wheel (or trying to) was one of the biggest mistakes when I started. In my naiveté, I bought as many different courses as I could and then tried to create my own new approach. I thought my new approach would be the "perfect" combination of stuff from five other people's courses. Can you guess what happened? Nothing.

Most people want the success others have had but resist the thought of modeling it. Have you ever felt this way? Success leaves clues. Despite this, you talk yourself out of modeling the path of someone successful by thinking, *"If he's doing it this way, then a lot of other people are doing it. I can't do that because then I'd be just like everybody else, so I'll just change things a bit and make it better."*

This is not the time to be a pioneer. Before you start changing things, wait until after you've been doing this a few years! Pioneers, as the saying goes, are the ones with all the arrows in their backs. The pioneers have already gone out there ahead of you. They've already shown you what works and what doesn't. Why are you trying to blaze a new trail and do things differently? Do you really think you can do it better? I've taken a lot of arrows for you, which is why this book even exists!

That said, I'm certainly not a "know it all" and don't know everything about everything. I'm just showing you what has worked for me and hundreds of my students. There is no need for you to reinvent the wheel — just model what works.

SUCCESS PRINCIPLE #3. TAKE THIS SERIOUSLY!!!

My editor may have an issue with my formatting on this one, but it's so important that I'm willing to violate grammar rules and put it in all caps with three exclamation points to boot.

In case you missed it, here it is again - TAKE THIS SERIOUSLY!!!

Wholesaling Lease Options can do wonders for your life but it makes for a really lousy hobby. You have to treat this like a business — a serious business. One of my early coaches would often tell me, *"Stop fartin' around and stop bein' a sissy."* Obviously, that's a G-rated, softer version of his advice — but I hope it drives home two points:

First, there's the "stop fartin' around" part. If you know what you need to do, just go do it. Don't get caught up in thinking you have to do a bunch of "busy work" and getting everything lined up in perfect order before you start taking any action. Forget all that and just do it.

Don't try to wait until you have steps 7-8 figured out before you start doing steps 1-2. Just focus on steps 1-2, and you will figure the rest out as you need it. That's why I created my Wholesaling Lease Options course. Learn more about my course in my free masterclass at WLOWebinar.com.

One of the phrases that get tossed around in the investment space is "Gun to your head, what would you decide?" That's not my favorite analogy - but suppose some psycho put a gun to your head and said, "You either send out these 100 letters to these sellers, or I'm going to shoot your head off." What would you do? I'll tell you what I'd do — I'd figure out how to write these letters... fast. I wouldn't get caught up in details. I'd just get it done.

If I didn't know what to say in the letters, I would go to this little known website (Google), and I would do an image search for "yellow letters". I would find about 20 billion examples of letters that I can copy.

The point is this... If you really wanted to send out these yellow letters, you would. You would go to Google, do a quick search, find a great example letter in 0.05 seconds, write it up, and send it out. You wouldn't worry about what color ink to use, what kind of yellow paper to use, what kind of font to use, what kind of stamp, etc, etc. Get the point?

Second, there's the "stop bein' a sissy" part. Most of this comes through marketing, or the lack thereof. Some people really hesitate to spend any money on marketing... Why? I have no idea. Do they hate making money? I don't know...

They're too afraid to spend a few hundred dollars on direct mail. But they'll gladly shell out tens of thousands of dollars on coaching, books, courses, or bootcamps. It's not that any of those things are bad — they can be very powerful tools - but only for the person that decides to take action. Otherwise, it's like owning a home gym set and never picking up the weights. None of this can make you stronger unless you decide to take action. The moment you decide to take action is the moment you start taking this business seriously.

Here's a bit of "word-nerd" insight: the root of the word **decide** is "cide" — which actually means "death". Homicide, suicide, fratricide, pesticide — these are all terms we are familiar with. The word "decide" quite literally means **"no other options"**. It's as if any other alternative is dead.

That's what happens when you **decide** to take this business seriously. You have killed off every other course of action. That doesn't mean everything will be perfect (more on that in the next principle), but it does mean you have resolved to move forward. You have decided to take this stuff seriously -- and that puts you in the top 1% of people out there.

SUCCESS PRINCIPLE #4. PROGRESS NOT PERFECTION

What am I getting at with this one? The answer lies in that crazy example earlier, the one about having a "gun to your head". In a situation like that, none of us would worry about perfection. We would just get the darn thing done.

This business is one of the worst places for "analysis paralysis". So many of us think we have to have everything completely worked out before we start... All our ducks have to be in a row. All of our questions must be answered. Everything has to be perfect before we take that first step.

Our desire for perfection is ultimately a sign of fear because deep down we are afraid of making mistakes. I hate to break the news but you are going to make mistakes. It's called life! You will make mistakes. Mistakes will find you. No two deals are ever the same. Every deal is always different, so you are never going to have it all figured out. You just need to accept that.

It is easy to listen to podcasts and get the impression that none of these people make mistakes. They still do, even to this day (including yours truly). What sets the winners apart is consistent action - progress... not perfection. Recognize that mistakes and failures are part of the game. Embrace them. "Fail forward fast", as they say.

SUCCESS PRINCIPLE #5. TAKE MASSIVE, IMPERFECT ACTION, EVERY DAY.

This principle might sound similar to #4, but here's the difference: Every Day.

There is a popular hashtag on social media right now (you know, those words you put the # sign in front of). It is #EveryDamnDay. Now, I don't use the word "damn" very often, but this hashtag is important... You do a lot of things every day — you eat every day, you brush your teeth every day, and you may even check social media like Facebook or LinkedIn every day.

If you have time for social media, you have time to make one or two phone calls… every single day. If you're tired of making phone calls, send out one or two letters every day.

Never let a day go by without taking some kind of action - no matter how small it is. That is how momentum starts.

Understand also that "massive action" doesn't necessarily mean making two-hundred calls and sending out a thousand letters within a 24-hour period. Suppose you have never done a deal before, or you are terrified to talk to sellers. If you just make one call to a seller every day, that is massive action.

Steps like these help you get in the habit of taking massive imperfect action. As long as you are taking action, it doesn't really matter if you do it perfect. This is all about progress.

From time to time, we all need someone in our lives to keep pushing us towards action. This is why I love coaching my students. If they make a mistake I simply say, *"Alright, you made a mistake. No worries. We will fix it. We can amend the contract, or negotiate a better deal, or we can just cancel the contract, or we can… fill-in-the-blank…"*

One of the tools I utilize with my clients is a scorecard. The scorecard starts with the amount of money the client wants to make. My first call with the client goes something like this: "All right, you want to make $10,000 a month? Cool... What kind of marketing are you going to do, consistently, every day? How many postcards are you going to send? How many texts or emails are you going to send, every day? How many sellers are you going to have to talk to every day? And how many offers are you going to make every day?"

Then I have them report on their numbers from the scorecard — every time I talk to them. The first thing I will ask, *"How much marketing did you do last week? How many sellers did you talk to? How many offers did you make?"*

You see - it's all about taking massive action - every day - even if it isn't perfect.

We all need some accountability. I don't necessarily have to be the one that coaches you. But I want you to understand that you need others to reinforce your commitment to massive, imperfect action — every day. Do this and you will create the momentum you need to carry forward.

SUCCESS PRINCIPLE #6.
STOP ASKING "WHAT IF?" AND START ASKING "WHAT'S NEXT?"

Having worked with hundreds of students the past few years, I've picked up on certain patterns that reflect a person's inner mindset. When you see the internal "programming" inside a person, it's almost always an indicator of whether they will succeed in this business — or not.

One of the biggest "tells" to a person's internal programming is in the kind of questions they ask. One of the most common I hear is "What if…?"

"What if" questions often reflect our inner fears and not the real issues. So instead I encourage my students to ask "What's next?"

This question keeps you forward focused. If you read the introduction to this book (which you should if you skipped it because it tells my back story and what you can learn from my experiences) — you'll remember that I asked a simple question: *"What do Wholesaling Lease Options make possible for me?"*

It is so easy to lose sight of the original reason you, me, and others have ventured out into this new world of flipping real estate by Wholesaling Lease Options. If success is sequential, that means you have to be focused on the next step in the sequence. You must stay forward focused.

Just today, I held a group coaching call for my students. There was a fair share of "What if" questions, but I put a time limit on that portion of the call so we always move into the "What's next" portion — which is infinitely more productive and fruitful.

Here are some better questions…

"Okay Joe, I have pulled a list and sent some letters. What happens next? What's next after I make an offer? What's happens after they say "No", do I follow-up?"

All of these questions (and their answers) build forward momentum. It also rewires the internal programming that can hinder so many of us. It's time to upgrade our software! Start asking "What's next?" instead of worrying about all the "What if's".

SUCCESS PRINCIPLE #7. DON'T ASK "HOW", ASK "WHO"

While it may seem smart to ask "how" questions — like *"How do I set up a website"*, *"How should I create my bandit signs"*, or *"How do I do the direct mail?"* — it's much better to ask "Who", as in "Who can do this for me?"

By now you know how strongly I believe in automation and delegation. There are a number of moving parts in setting up this business: websites, CRMs (customer relationship management systems), and talking with sellers. These tasks may seem huge and be intimidating at first glance - as though they were a towering, awe-inspiring monument, like the six-hundred thirty foot Gateway Arch in my hometown of St. Louis.

But it is my job to show you a path forward that can give you margin and freedom. Naturally, I get some resistance to outsourcing because people wonder why they should spend money on tasks they can do themselves. The little detail tasks (like doing websites or entering data into your CRM) are important, they just shouldn't be important to YOU.

That's $5 per hour activity. You need to be focused on $500 per hour activity.

What are your highest revenue generating activities? It isn't creating a website, updating your CRM, sending text to follow-up with sellers, etc.

It is making offers. That's it. You shouldn't be focused on anything else. Your speed to income is directly proportional to the number of offers you make.

If you want to do a lot of deals, you need to make lots of offers. Everything else… automate and delegate… or die.

Outsourcing is absolutely vital to your long-term success. Recently one student asked me how to mail mass letters from home, and whether they should be tri-fold or four-fold. I didn't even answer his question. Instead I asked him a question. Can you guess what it was?

"How many offers did you make in the last week?"

Guess what his answer was? *"None. I am still trying to get my direct mail out the door."*

Okay, I get it… You need to send the mail first. But why hasn't he done it yet? Why is he wasting time trying to do it himself, and wondering how many times the paper should be folded?! I told him to get a printing company to do it. See, printing and sending letters is a $5 an hour job. This guy should have been doing the $500 an hour jobs.

Step away from all the "details", and put your time to it's highest and best use. You need to talk to sellers and make offers. These are the most valuable tasks. Nothing else matters. That's all you should focus on. Get someone else to do everything else for you.

YOU NEED TO WATCH MY FREE MASTERCLASS AND BUY MY COURSE

I have to tell you something… If you're at all half way interested in Wholesaling Lease Option deals, you need to attend my masterclass and buy my course.

I don't know what else to say to convince you. But here are several simple reasons why…

1. There is simply no better course out there on how to flip lease options. None.

2. My Wholesaling Lease Options strategy is the easiest and fastest way to make money in real estate today.

3. It can help you to quit your job and make a full-time income in real estate, in 90 days or less.

4. It's easy…

5. You can do these deals virtually, from a cafe in Prague, a beach in Spain, or your own backyard…All you need is a laptop and a phone.

Go watch my free masterclass right now at WLOWebinar.com.

I appreciate you all

5

WORK SMARTER NOT HARDER - PARTNER WITH ME

In this chapter, I share with you about how you can work smarter, not harder by partnering with me on deals. If you want to get to your goals faster, you can work with me one-on-one.

Now, if you just want my course, you can go to wlowebinar.com and watch my free masterclass. The course goes over everything we have talked about in this book in detail. You can attend the class at wlowebinar.com.

We are looking for a select group of partners to work with one-on-one. These partners will start with a completely new wholesaling lease options business in new cities across the country. Our team and I wholesaled about 6 properties in the last week and about 22 deals in the last 4 months. Our team grossed over $100,000 in wholesaling profits. But we want to do more deals.

If you already doing lease option deals, then this is for you and I want you to pay attention here. This is not just about coaching or mentoring.

My team and I are looking for several select partners that we can personally work with to open new markets and launch a completely new wholesaling lease options business from scratch. So, if you are struggling to get your business off the ground or you are tired of doing this alone then this may be the opportunity you have been waiting for.

WHAT WE WILL PROVIDE FOR YOU

Let me describe what we will provide for you. We are going to personally help you set up the entire wholesaling lease options business from scratch.

As a partner, you work with me and my team personally. You will be getting on the phone with us regularly each week, perhaps even daily, to successfully do deals in your market.

The partnership starts with you scheduling a personal office visit with me and my team in St. Louis. While you are here, we set up your systems and schedule all your marketing for you. We do your market research, create a marketing plan and then implement the marketing plan. This is by far one of the most valuable aspects of our program and something no one else is doing.

Now, the number of people that we can work in each market is extremely limited and this is strictly on a first come first serve basis.

We research your market and find exactly where the demand is located. We build an active buyers list and find the best sellers to market to in your market. We create and then implement a solid marketing plan which will get your phone ringing within weeks. We are going to help you pull our unique seller list for direct mail, cold calling, voice blast, etc.

The other thing that we are going to be doing is getting all your systems up and running. We are talking about your buyer and seller websites, your CRM database, your phone systems, your direct mail campaigns, cold calling systems, Craigslist and Zillow scraping and texting.

We also hire your first virtual assistant for you who can help you with marketing, updating the CRM database, updating your scorecard, pulling comps, property details, as well as sending follow-up offers and letters to sellers. Your virtual assistant can also add sellers to your email autoresponders and send voice blasts to old leads.

Your virtual assistant is mainly helping you with the follow-up, so you won't be spending needless time behind the computer trying to remember everything you need to do… the virtual assistant is going to be able to do that stuff for you.

We also help you get cash buyers. You can get access to our cash if you need it to close on a deal. You also get access to our national database of cash buyers. If we can't close it or you don't want to close it, we will find somebody else that will. I know a lot of people all over the country. We provide support, hands-on coaching, and sales training to structure offers and close deals.

You will work personally with me and my business partner Gavin. We are going to communicate regularly primarily through the app Voxer. We have weekly coaching calls, a premium private Facebook group and anything else required to get your business up and running.

Our marketing strategy and systems are working in today's market. These are the same tools that we are using in our business today to wholesale multiple properties every week. We know they work. We share them with our partners...and only our partners.

WHAT YOU WILL BE DOING
(Under Our Guidance And Supervision)

Here is what you will be doing under our guidance and supervision. You will review new leads as they come in and calling them back immediately. You make appointments with owners to look at the properties and take photos and videos. You also do the following

- Make offers on all your leads
- Follow-up with sellers
- Network with cash buyers
- Update your databases of tenant buyers
- Follow-up on future potential deals

Our goal is to help you focus on what gives you the best return of your time and money. You focus on talking to sellers and making offers... not on doing the marketing and techy stuff.

REQUIREMENTS

We do have some requirements for you to be our partner. You need to be a fast implementor. We only want to work with someone who quickly implements what they learn. If you are afraid to take decisive massive action, afraid to make a mistake or need to have all your questions answered before you will take action, then do not apply. We want a "ready, fire, aim" person.

Also, you need to be able to devote 3 - 4 hours a day to do real estate. You need good communication skills. If you are the type of person that needs extreme hand holding and has to have everything spelled out for you in excruciating detail... then this is not probably for you.

We are looking for entrepreneurs. We do not want to be babysitters. If you are interested, you need to go to coachjoe.net to get more information and fill out an application.

INVESTMENT REQUIRED

This partnership requires an investment from you for marketing and systems. You need a marketing budget of at least $5000 to cover the first 3 months to get you started. We would like to schedule all the marketing out for 3 months to ensure consistency.

We also have our "are you serious about this" deposit. It is like an investment insurance policy. We do not care about the money, it is just a deposit. You have to pay this upfront to show us that you are serious and willing to compensate us in doing all the work in setting up the business for you. Remember this. It is important. You are going to get this money credited back to you when you do your first one or two deals.

So, again we are not here for the coaching fees, we are in this to do more deals. The reason for this fee is to make sure you are serious and not going to waste our time or perhaps disappear after 1 month. We are not in the business of pushing a parked car. This deposit is in addition to the marketing money that you will need as indicated above.

We do not guarantee results. We are not making any income claims. You should be able to make all that money back within your first two or three deals. And you should look at this fee as an investment that is only a small percentage of what you should be making every year.

If your pinching pennies then this is probably not for you. We are looking for serious players that have money to invest. If you are broke, please do not apply. But if you are serious action taker then let's get started. You can apply at coachjoe.net.

HOW TO APPLY (Serious Inquiries Only)

How to apply? If you go to coachjoe.net, you will read the information and see a video with more information about this program. You will see everything that I have just said here at coachjoe.net.

One important thing to note is that the application process is the only way to be considered in the position. So, go to coachjoe.net to fill out that application.

Once you fill it out, we will review it and send you a text message or give you a call. We also may call you right away. So, please be ready to make a decision and understand that we will choose only those people that we think are going to be a good fit. So if you think you had what it takes then go to coachjoe.net.

This is available only to people in a few select markets. We don't put multiple people in one market.

Partnering with me may not be for you. If you are not interested in partnering then you can focus on learning how to do wholesaling lease options. You can make a full time income doing it and hopefully quit your job in 3 months just like I did. Go watch my class at wlowebinar.com.

If you want to partner with us and do deals with us, go to coachjoe.net. Watch the video, read that page and fill out the application. We will contact you to see if you are a good fit.

HAVE YOU CHECKED OUT MY PODCAST?

If you have not heard of my podcast yet, go check it out at RealEstateInvestingMastery.com. I have been doing this podcast for over 7 years now, I have 3 million downloads with over 600 episodes.

It just blows my mind that this little podcast that I have been doing has been a downloaded so many times from people all over the world. And it is really a passion of mine. I teach and I give a ton of free stuff in the podcast. It is beneficial for you to check it out.

Again, the podcast is called Real Estate Investing Mastery. You can find it at RealEstateInvestingMastery.com or do a search on Google Play, iTunes, Stitcher, or TuneIn Radio.

ABOUT THE AUTHOR

Joe McCall is an avid family guy who enjoys hanging out with his kids at the zoo or golfing with his boys or swimming with his girls in the pool. Nothing is more important to Joe than God and family.

Joe has flipped hundreds of deals and helped students flip thousands more. He loves doing deals and helping his students do the same. He has been fortunate to receive more student testimonials than he can count.

He invests remotely in multiple markets. He loves creating automated marketing systems. He has a popular podcast called The Real Estate Investing Mastery Podcast.

While living in Prague, Czech Republic (twice, for several months) and traveling across the northwest corner of the United States in his RV for three months, his teams have flipped multiple lease options and regular wholesale deals—without him seeing the house or talking to the sellers or the buyers—ever.

Joe believes that the greatest part of this business is that he gets the privilege of working wherever and whenever he wants—from home, from Starbucks, the pool, a condo in Colorado, a coffee shop in Prague, a farmhouse in Ireland—wherever!

RESOURCES

If you need help wholesaling lease options, check out my resources below.

- Blog:
  joemccall.com

- Best-selling podcast:
  realestateinvestingmastery.com

- FREE Lease Options Contract:
  simpleleaseoptions.com

- Free Training on Wholesaling Lease Options:
  wlowebinar.com

- Free Wholesaling 101 Mindmap:
  flipmindmap.com

- Partner With Me On Deals:
  coachjoe.net

- Website:
  wholesalingleaseoptions.com